FLORAL FRAGRANCES

Text by Hilary Walden
Illustrations by Mary Woodin

CRESCENT BOOKS

Editorial Direction: Joanna Lorenz
Art Direction: Bobbie Colgate-Stone
Production Control: Susan Brown
Hand Lettering: Leonard Currie

First published in 1990 by Pyramid Books,
an imprint of the Octopus Publishing Group,
Michelin House, 81 Fulham Road, London SW3 6RB.

This 1990 edition published by Crescent Books,
distributed by Outlet Book Company, Inc.,
a Random House Company,
225 Park Avenue South, New York,
New York 10003.

Printed and bound in Spain

ISBN 0–517–03083–7

87654321

CONTENTS

Introduction	4	Frozen Flower Ice Bowl	34
A Lavender Bag	8.	Lily-of-the-Valley Handcream	36
Orange Blossom Moisturizer	10	Restoring Limeflower Oil	38
Sweet Pea Steam Facial	12	Scented Rose Petal Soap	40
Hyacinth Flower Candle	14	A Pretty Floral Garter	42
Scented Flowery Honey	16	Floral Room Fragrance	44
Lilac Washing Lather	18	Fragrant Rose Pink Syrup	46
Elderflower & Gooseberry Jelly	20	Violet Flower Sorbet	48
Soothing Cornflower Compress	22	Elderflower Champagne	50
Chamomile Oatmeal Scrub	24	Honeysuckle Ointment	52
Scented Drawer Lining Paper	26	Bath Sachet of Hyacinth	54
Floral Toilet Water	28	Fragrant Chamomile Hair Rinse	56
Freesia Petal Bath Oil	30	Traditional Rose Junket	58
Jasmine Furniture Polish	32	Lime Flower Lotion	60
		Violet Cleansing Milk	62

$\mathcal{I}$NTRODUCTION

THE INIMITABLE, FRESH fragrances of flowers are a major element of their attraction and charm. In the following pages you will find many delightful ways to capture and save those evocative scents, in a wide range of home-made, natural products that are a joy both to use and to give as presents that cannot fail to bring pleasure.

For centuries, people have taken advantage of the fragrances of flowers to improve every aspect of their lives – in gentle cosmetics to cleanse and beautify the body and complexion, to add enticing flavours to food and drinks, to make pure remedies to cure or combat minor ailments, and to clean and perfume the home and clothes. As well as being used for their perfuming powers, many flowers have age-old reputations for being valuable in other ways; lavender, for example, has a calming effect, rose products soothe the skin, orange flower water is good for oily complexions, elderflowers cure dandruff, and chamomile brightens and highlights the colour of fair hair. If these powers are not required, the flowers used in the following pages can be replaced by other fragrant ones of your choice.

When using flowers in food as flavouring or decoration, in drinks, or in medicaments that are to be taken internally, only use flowers that you are absolutely certain are safe, and follow instructions accurately, paying particular attention to quantities. Always avoid any that have been treated with insecticides, pesticides or herbicides, or which have grown near a road. If you pick flowers growing wild, check that the land does not belong to anyone, and if it does, ask their permission. Never strip a plant, clump or patch bare and leave rare plants alone.

Whichever flowers you use, choose those that are free from blemishes and damage, and pick them in the morning of a dry day, after the dew has vanished but before the sun is too hot.

THE LANGUAGE OF FLOWERS

Many flowers have been credited with special meanings of their own for hundreds of years, but it was during the Victorian era that sending messages with flowers, to suitors and friends, became perfected and fashionable.

Almond blossom – hope
Anemone – forsakeness
Bluebell – constancy
Camelia – excellence
Carnation, red – alas, for my poor heart

Carnation, striped – refusal

Chrysanthemum, red – I love you

Daisy – innocence

Honeysuckle – devotion

Hyacinth, blue – constancy

Jasmine, white – amiability

Jasmine, yellow – happiness, grace and elegance

Lavender – silence

Lilac, white – modesty

Lily – purity

Magnolia – grief

Michaelmas daisy – farewell

Poppy, red – consolation

Rose – love

Snowdrop – hope

Tulip – love

Violet – modesty

Wallflower – fidelity in adversity

A LAVENDER BAG

The natural old-fashioned, tried and tested method of keeping clothes smelling sweet and fresh, and warding off moths.
Cut a piece of pretty, fine-weave natural material into a square. With the right sides together, sew up three of the sides. Turn the material right side out, and fill with dried lavender flowers. Sew up the remaining side, incorporating a length of appropriately coloured ribbon to hang up the bag. Decorate with broderie anglaise or eyelet lace, a ruffle or frill, embroidery or appliqué work.

pretty fabric

lavender

9

ORANGE BLOSSOM MOISTURIZER

This scented face cream gives smooth, fresh-looking skin.

Pour ³/4 cup of boiling water over a heaped tablespoon of fresh, or ¹/2 tablespoon dried, orange blossoms. Cover and leave for 15 minutes. Strain off the water, pressing the flowers well. Melt a ¹/3 cup of beeswax with a cup of almond oil in a bowl placed over a saucepan of hot water, stirring occasionally until smooth. Lift the bowl from the pan, then, very gradually, beat in the orange blossom water with a wooden spoon. Put into jars when cool.

orange blossom

beeswax

11

Sweet Pea
Steam Facial

~

*The gently fragrant vapour deeply cleanses the
skin by opening the pores and lifting
out impurities.
Put 4 heaped tablespoons of fresh sweet pea petals
into a bowl or basin. Pour boiling water over them,
bend over the basin so your face is a short distance
above the water, then drape a towel over your head
and the basin to form a tent. Allow your skin to
steam gently for 10 minutes.*

sweet peas

13

HYACINTH
FLOWER CANDLE

In a bowl placed over a saucepan of hot water, melt some chopped candles. Crush a cupful of fresh hyacinth flowers, then tie them in a muslin bag. Put into the wax, cover the bowl and leave for 40 minutes. Remove the bag. If necessary, add a few drops of candlemakers' perfuming oil and colouring before pouring into moulds with wicks fitted. Leave to set, topping up the wells that form around the wicks with molten wax. Remove the moulds, and leave the candles in a warm, dry place for several days to harden. Decorate with pressed flowers held in place with a small dab of clear adhesive.

hyacinth
flowers

SCENTED
FLOWERY HONEY

*Gently melt 1¼ cups of good mild honey in a
bowl placed over a saucepan of gently boiling
water. Lightly bruise a cup of fragrant fresh flower
petals (such as honeysuckle or rose), stir into the
honey, and heat gently for half an hour.
Remove from the heat, cover and stand in a warm
place for a week, stirring occasionally. Reheat
gently, then strain through cheesecloth into clean
jars, cover, and label.*

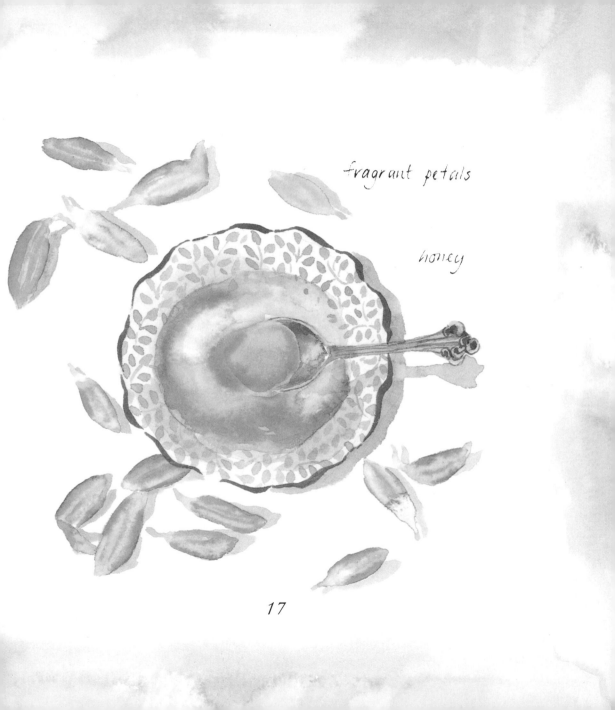

fragrant petals

honey

17

LILAC WASHING LATHER

*Use this lotion for washing delicate fabrics, to
make them soft and to give them a beautiful sheen
and lasting feminine fragrance.
Boil a bunch of crushed soapwort leaves and 3 to 4
tablespoons of fresh lilac florets in about 1¼ cups
of rainwater, or soft water, for 3 to 4 minutes.
Remove from the heat, cover and leave until cold.
Press through a sieve, and pour the liquid into a
screw-top bottle. Use enough of the lotion to form
a lather in hand-hot water.*

soapwort

lilac

19

ELDERFLOWER &
GOOSEBERRY JELLY

Simmer 2 lb (1.2 kg) of gooseberries, 3¾ cups of water and 2 large fresh elderflower heads in a large saucepan, until the berries are very soft. Strain through a jelly bag or sieve lined with several thicknesses of cheesecloth, allowing the juice to drip naturally – do not press it through. Measure the clear juice into a pan and for each 2½ cups, add 2 cups of warmed sugar. Heat gently, stirring, until the sugar has dissolved, then add 2 more large elderflower heads and boil for 15 minutes, until setting point. Remove the flowers and scum and pour into warmed sterilized pots.

gooseberries

elderflower

21

Soothing
Cornflower Compress

*To soothe tired eyes and bring back their sparkle.
Mix together a tablespoon of fresh rose petals and
a tablespoon of fresh cornflowers, or a teaspoon of
dried ones, then boil in a cup of distilled water for
5 minutes. Cover and leave to cool before straining
off the liquid. Dip muslin or cotton pads into the
liquid and place over the eyes; lie down and
relax for 10 minutes.*

dried
cornflowers

rose
petals

23

CHAMOMILE
OATMEAL SCRUB

A scrub to thoroughly cleanse oily skins and leave them glowing. Make as required.

First prepare 1 tablespoon of strong fresh or dried chamomile infusion. Grind 2/3 cup of oatmeal to a fine powder then mix with 1 tablespoon of the infusion and about 3 tablespoons of warm milk, to make a paste. Gently rub over the face avoiding the eyes. Rinse off with warm water.

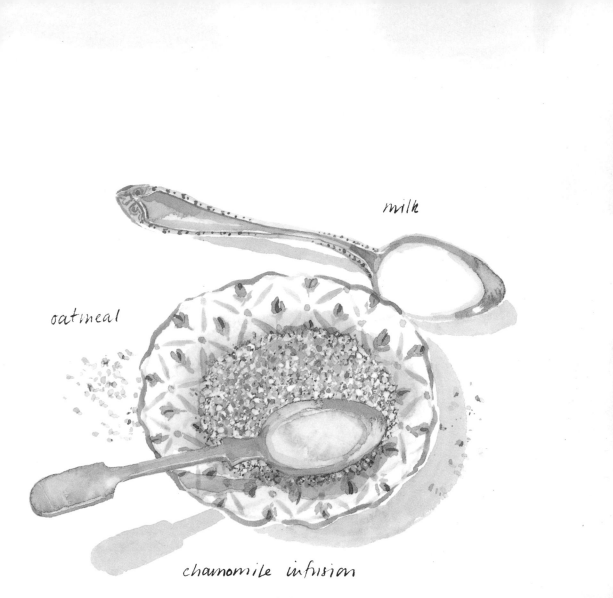

milk

oatmeal

chamomile infusion

25

Scented Drawer Lining Paper

Scatter a good layer of dry pot pourri mixture in a box that is large enough to hold the sheets of lining paper. Lay the paper in the box, scattering more pot pourri in between the sheets. Cover the box and leave in a cool place for at least 6 weeks, for the paper to absorb the fragrance.

lining paper

pot pourri

FLORAL
TOILET WATER

Fill a warmed, heatproof jar with scented fresh or dried flowers or petals of your choice. Cover with boiling water (measuring the amount you add), cover or close the jar and leave to cool slightly. Add 2 tablespoons of flavourless alcohol or vodka for every 4½ cups (or litre) of water. Cover or close again and leave to become completely cold. Strain through fine muslin, and pour into bottles, for preference ones with ground glass stoppers.

dried petals

29

Freesia Petal
Bath Oil

~

Pack crushed fresh freesias to within an inch (2.5 cm) of the top of a jar, then fill the jar with warm mild olive oil. Cover and leave in a sunny or warm place for about 3 weeks, shaking the jar once or twice daily. Gently warm the jar slightly in a saucepan of hot water then strain through a cheesecloth-lined sieve. Use this oil to repeat the process 2 or 3 times, using fresh petals each time, until the oil is well perfumed. Strain through a double thickness of cheesecloth before pouring into a bottle with a ground glass stopper.

freesias

JASMINE FURNITURE POLISH

*Add a gentle floral fragrance to furniture at the
same time as making it shine, and so make a
whole room smell welcoming.*
*Grate beeswax into a screw-top jar. Cover with
turpentine, close the lid, and leave for at least 2
weeks, shaking the jar occasionally, and adding a
little more turpentine as necessary to give a smooth
paste consistency. Stir in a few drops of
jasmine essential oil.*

jasmine

beeswax

FROZEN FLOWERY ICE BOWL

This makes a pretty presentation bowl for iced desserts. Boil and cool some water. Pour about 1/3 inch (1 cm) into a freezerproof bowl, arrange fresh attractive flowers in the water then stand, level, in the freezer until the water is frozen. Cover the iced flowers with more boiled and cooled water, freeze, then place in a smaller, weighted bowl on the centre on the ice. Pour water between the bowls and freeze. Wipe inside the inner bowl with a hot cloth, carefully twist and remove the bowl. Re-warm the cloth, wipe the outer bowl and carefully lift it away. Return the ice bowl to the freezer.

34

fresh flowers

35

LILY-OF-THE-VALLEY
HANDCREAM

Rub this lightly fragrant cream into your hands to keep them soft and supple.

Gently melt ½ cup of petroleum jelly in a bowl placed over a saucepan of hot water. Using a wooden spoon, stir in 3 to 4 heaped tablespoons of crushed fresh lily-of-the-valley flowers, cover and keep over hot water for 30 minutes. Strain the jelly. Add a few drops of lily-of-the-valley essential oil, if necessary, then pour into warm pots. When cold, cover and label.

lily-of-the-valley

Restoring
Limeflower Oil

*Massage this oil firmly into tired and weary feet
and legs to restore them.
Tightly pack as many fresh limeflowers as possible
into a screw-top jar. Cover with almond oil and
close the lid. Leave in a sunny warm place for 2 to
3 weeks, shaking the jar every other day.
Pour the oil and flowers into a wide, thick-
bottomed saucepan and heat until the flowers are
crisp. Cool slightly, then strain into warmed
bottles. When cold, cover and label.*

lime flowers

almond oil

39

SCENTED

ROSE PETAL SOAP

Pure, mild and fragrant.
Melt 10 tablespoons of finely grated castille soap
with 8 tablespoons of water in a bowl placed over
a saucepan of hot water, stirring frequently until
evenly blended. Crush 2 tablespoons of dried rose
petals to a fine powder and stir into the soap with
4 drops of rose oil. Strain into warmed jars and
leave to cool before covering and labelling.

castille soap

dried rose petals

41

A Pretty Floral Garter

*This whimsical gift is for decoration, really.
You need a length of elastic that will not be too
tight, and a strip of pretty fine linen, lawn or voile
that is double the length of the elastic, and two
and a half times as wide. With the reverse sides
facing out, fold the fabric length in half and sew
up the long sides. Turn the fabric right side out,
and make a line of stitches just inside the long
edges. Thread the elastic through. Hold one short
end closed, with a clothes-peg or clothes-pin for
example, open out the other end and drop in
scented dried flowers. Sew the short ends together.*

42

fine linen

dried flowers

43

Floral Room Fragrance

~

Stir together 6 tablespoons each of crushed fresh lavender flowers, 3 tablespoons of finely crushed cloves and finely crushed cinnamon; and 2 tablespoons each of orris root and gum benzoin powder. Blend together ½ tablespoon each of essential oils of bergamot, clove, sweet orange and rose, then thoroughly mix into the lavender mixture. Keep in a tightly closed glass jar, in a cool, dark place, for some time to allow the ingredients to mature and meld together. Transfer to a metal dish and place above a radiator or in a warm, sunny spot.

lavender

cloves

cinnamon

45

FRAGRANT

ROSE PINK SYRUP

Dilute this syrup with sparkling mineral water, soda water or tonic, or mix with hot water and perhaps a dash of brandy to soothe and warm you. You can also make an enticing cocktail by adding to dry white wine or sparkling wine.

Gently heat 1/2 cup of sugar in 1 1/4 cups of water, stirring with a wooden spoon until dissolved. Add a strip of lemon rind and simmer for 10 minutes. Off the heat, discard the lemon and stir in a handful of crushed fresh clove pink petals. Cover and leave in a fairly warm place for a day. Transfer to somewhere cool until cold, then strain.

46

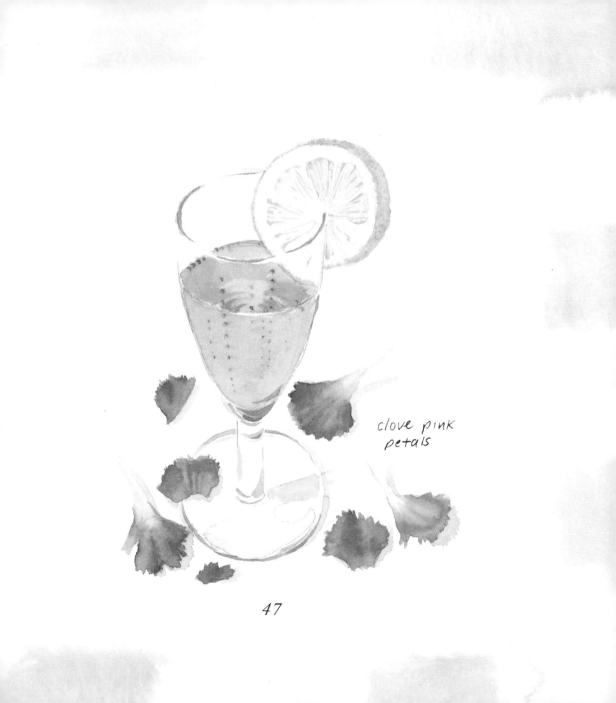

clove pink
petals

47

VIOLET

FLOWER SORBET

~

Gently heat 1¼ cups of sugar in 2½ cups of water
until dissolved, then boil until the syrup feels
sticky. Pour half the syrup into a container. Add
the strained juice of 1 lemon and ⅓ cup of fresh
violets to the syrup in the pan, boil for 30 seconds
then leave to steep for 8 hours. Strain and briefly
purée with the remaining syrup and another ⅓ cup
of violets. If flavour is weak, too sweet or needs
'lifting', add a few drops of violet oil, or some
lemon juice. Pour into a shallow metal container
and freeze until firm, stirring from the sides to the
centre several times.

sorbet

violets

49

ELDERFLOWER
CHAMPAGNE

A fragrant, refreshing summer drink –
though not alcoholic!
Dissolve 3½ cups of sugar in 2 cups of hot water.
Pour into a non-metallic container with 4 large
fresh elderflower heads, 2 tablespoons of white wine
vinegar, the juice of 1 lemon, the lemon rind
(without the pith), cut into quarters, and 18 cups
(4 litres) of water. Stir, cover and leave
for 4 to 5 days. Strain off the liquid into clean,
screw-top bottles, and leave for 6 days or until
effervescing. Serve chilled.

lemon

elderflowers

51

HONEYSUCKLE OINTMENT

This lovely scented ointment can be used to bring gentle soothing relief to minor burns and sunburn. Gently bring 1/2 cup of petroleum jelly to the boil with about 3 heaped tablespoons of crushed fresh honeysuckle flowers, then simmer for 20 minutes, stirring occasionally. Strain into warmed jars and leave to cool before covering and labelling.

honeysuckle
flowers

BATH SACHET
OF HYACINTH

Cut a piece of pretty, closely woven cloth or cheesecloth to a circle approximately 7 inches (18 cm) in diameter. Hem around the edge. Place about 3 tablespoons of dried hyacinth florets in the centre, then fold up the sides and gather together just below the edge. Wind and tie securely a long length of ribbon or cord around to make a 'dolly bag'. Suspend the bag from the hot tap, well down into the bath, so the water flows through it.

fabric and ribbon

hyacinth flowers

FRAGRANT
CHAMOMILE HAIR RINSE

To brighten dull hair and leave it smelling good.
Put ¹/₂ cup of dried chamomile flowers into a
saucepan with 2¹/₂ cups of water. Bring to the boil
then simmer for 15 minutes. Strain through muslin
onto a cup containing fresh, scented petals. Stir,
cover and leave for 30 minutes. Strain again
and warm to use.

fresh petals

dried chamomile
flowers

Traditional
Rose Junket

*A simple yet elegant, delicious
and attractive dessert.
Stir 2 teaspoons of caster or fine granulated sugar
into 2½ cups of milk and warm gently in a
saucepan to blood heat (tepid to the touch).
Flavour with a few drops of rose water, and colour
a delicate pink with a little edible food colouring, if
liked. Stir in 3 teaspoons of rennet and pour into a
pretty glass dish. Leave quite still at room
temperature to set, 2 to 3 hours. Carefully pour a
layer of double or heavy cream over the surface
just before serving and decorate with rose petals.*

rose junket

59

LIME FLOWER LOTION

For removing the last traces of soap or cleanser, closing pores and refining the skin's texture. Gently boil 3 to 4 heaped tablespoons of dried lime flowers in ½ cup of water in a covered saucepan for 20 minutes. Cool slightly, then pour through a strainer, pressing down well on the flowers. Pour the liquid into bottles with ground glass stoppers or screw-caps, and label.

lime flowers

Violet Cleansing Milk

For cleansing oily skins gently but thoroughly. Put 3 heaped tablespoons of fresh violet flowers into a bowl placed over a saucepan of hot water. Add 1¼ cups milk heated to just below simmering point. Cover and leave over heat until the milk smells strongly of violets, stirring gently from time to time. Strain the milk into a screw-topped bottle. Keep in a cold place and use within 2 to 3 days.

violets .

Hilary Walden has written many books on flowers, crafts, food, and wine; she contributes regularly to magazines and newspapers, and broadcasts on radio and television, on these and other subjects.

Mary Woodin received her Master of Arts from the Royal College of Art in London before working as an illustrator and ceramic designer; among other projects she has designed china for Wedgwood and tiles for the new-look London Underground.